TIAN WEN

A Chinese Book of Origins

Tian Wen

A CHINESE BOOK
OF ORIGINS

Translated with an introduction by
Stephen Field

A NEW DIRECTIONS BOOK

Portions of this translation first appeared in *PN Review* #40 in 1984.

Manufactured in the United States of America
First published clothbound and as New Directions Paperbook 624
in 1986
Published simultaneously in Canada by Penguin Books
Canada Limited

LIBRARY OF CONGRESS CATALOGING-IN-PUBLICATION DATA

Ch'ü, Yüan, ca. 343–ca. 277 B.C.
    Tian wen: a Chinese book of origins.
        (A New Directions Book)
    Translation of T'ien wen.
    Includes bibliographical references.
    I. Field, Stephen.   II. Title.
PL2661.T5E5   1986   895.1'11   86-12737
ISBN 0-8112-1010-3
ISBN 0-8112-1011-1 (pbk.)

NEW DIRECTIONS BOOKS ARE PUBLISHED FOR JAMES LAUGHLIN
BY NEW DIRECTIONS PUBLISHING CORPORATION,
80 EIGHTH AVENUE, NEW YORK 10011

To the memory of
Roy E. Teele,
Scholar, Mentor, and Friend

ACKNOWLEDGMENTS

I am deeply grateful to three Austin scholars whose aid proved invaluable in various stages of this translation: Jeannette Faurot, Christopher Middleton, and Carl Rubino. I also wish to express my gratitude to Burton Watson for his comments on reading the final translation. Any mistakes or omissions are my own. Lastly I would like to acknowledge the memory of Roy Teele whose class first introduced me to *Tian wen*, and who offered to read the final draft of the translation and make suggestions before he passed away on December 5, 1985.   S. F.

The *Tian wen* is recognizably one of the most baffling works of poetry in the classical Chinese tradition, attracting in its 2300-year history an average of one scholarly analysis every twenty years. Although relatively unknown in the West, it remains the most comprehensive single catalogue of ancient Chinese mythology and pre-imperial legend. Yet by the time the poem was collected in the *Chu ci* (Songs of Chu) by the Eastern Han dynasty scholar, Wang Yi (died 158 A.D.), the meaning of a great many of the verses had already been lost.

Wang Yi reported that Qu Yuan, a high minister of the southern state of Chu (died *c.* 288 B.C.), unjustly banished by the king because of slander, composed the work in the Chu ancestral temples. The walls of the royal shrines were said to be painted with murals of the scenes depicted in the poem, and the loyal statesman in his dejection adopted a tone of mocking skepticism. Wang's fanciful story of the poem's origin is now generally discounted for reasons as obvious as the inordinate number of murals necessary and the location of the temples in a place of banishment. Even though Qu Yuan is credited with the composition of the major works that form the *Chu ci* (such as the *Li sao*, or "Encountering Sorrow"), it is unlikely that he created the *Tian wen* in its entirety.

One reason for this is the total absence of "breathing sounds" in the poem. A characteristic of all other songs attributed to Qu Yuan is the presence in odd-numbered lines of the breathing particle *xi*—an otherwise meaningless sound that originally adapted the lyrics to the melody of the song. This particle is also common in the folk songs of the *Shi jing* (Book of Odes)—the earlier and perhaps better known Chinese anthology—and is translated as the balladic "O" in my rendition of the refrain in Ode no. 72:

> She gathers there the wormwood, O!
> One day without the sight of her
>   Is like a long three autumns, O!

Yet no instance of *xi* occurs in the *Tian wen*. Besides separating the poem from other more emotive songs in the Chu anthology, this absence also serves to solemnify the mood.

Although possibly less lyrical, the work is not less literary than the "sao" form, as various modern scholars would have us believe. The rhythm of the poem is exceptionally regular, for the most part consisting of an eight-character line broken in the middle by a caesura, resulting in a tetrasyllabic meter. I have translated the eight-syllable Chinese line into an English couplet. Successive lines in the *Tian wen* rhyme, which would thus correspond to rhyming couplets in English. Although the narrative value of individual questions usually occupies the length of two lines in the Chinese original, still, a query is sometimes complete in as little as four characters. On the other hand, in one instance a story continues for a space of twelve lines. For this reason I have numbered couplets in the translation, and the reader is free to link as many as the narrative demands.

Precisely because the poem is devoid of a single all-encompassing narrative theme, which would allow the work to stand alone as "story," modern scholars have been puzzled as to the purpose for its creation. Not even the meaning of the title is without controversy. Since verbs and nouns are indistinguishable outside the context of a sentence in Chinese, the expression "*tian wen*" can be rendered "Heaven asks" and "Heaven's questions," on the one hand, or "asking Heaven" and "questions about Heaven," on the other. Since the first twenty-two couplets of the poem are concerned with the origin of celestial phenomena, I am inclined to believe the title originally pertained to just those questions and meant something like, "Investigation of the Heavens."

The format of the poem, a rapid succession of enigmatic questions or riddles, is almost unique in the annals of ancient Chinese literature. Still, one remarkably similar poem exists in a roughly contemporaneous work, the philosophical text known as the *Zhuangzi*. The second of two seminal Taoist classics, this thirty-three-chapter work is attributed to the historical Zhuang Zhou (*c.* 365–290 B.C.) of the southern state of Song. It consists of three traditional sections: the "Inner Chapters" (1–7), believed to represent the authentic sayings of the historic Zhuangzi, or Master Zhuang, plus the "Outer" (8–22) and "Miscellaneous Chapters" (23–33). At the beginning of Chapter 14, *Tian Yun* ("The Turning of Heaven"), can be found the following poem:

> Heaven, does it revolve?
> And Earth, does it sit still?
> The sun and moon, do they jostle for position?
> Who draws the bow that fires them?

Who ties the net that holds them?
Who rests with nothing to do,
    Yet gives the push that moves them?

Is there perhaps some locked-in motion
    So they have no other alternative?
Do they just spin around and round
    Unable to stop of their own accord?

The clouds, do they make rain?
Or the rains, do they make clouds?
Who swells them up and releases them?
Who rests with nothing to do,
    Yet stirs them up with overflowing joy?

The winds rise in the north,
Blowing west and blowing east,
Then whirl around up high.
Who inhales and breathes them out?
Who rests with nothing to do,
    Yet shakes them off and brushes them about?

Although this poem is collected in the "Outer Chapters" in the extant version of the *Zhuangzi*, an eighth-century Buddhist text cites it from the "Inner Chapters," and A. C. Graham[1] subsequently places it in Chapter 2, after Zhuangzi's famous parable of the wind. The form and content of this poem is so similar to that of the *Tian wen* that it is tempting to try to relate them.

In the attempt to shed light on this poem it is necessary to recall still one more passage from the *Zhuangzi*, this time from Chapter 33, *Tian Xia* ("Under Heaven"). There was an "unusual" man named Huang Liao from the South who asked Hui Shi, the logician, two questions: why does Heaven not topple and Earth not sink, and what is the origin of wind, rain, and rolling thunder? The philosopher answered in his characteristic fashion—at great length—concluding with an astonishing statement, most likely a paradox. Nowhere else is the strange Southerner, Huang, mentioned, nor is it explained why he is considered unusual, but his questions are remarkably similar to Zhuangzi's poem. Unfortunately Hui Shi's answer is not specifically recorded, or we might have an idea how the enigmatic questions of the *Tian wen* were answered by hair-splitting dialecticians.

There is evidence to support the view that the discussion between Huang Liao and Hui Shi was not an isolated encounter. The Warring States kingdom of Qi, in the vicinity of present-day Shandong Province, was one of the most powerful of the seven contending states, and during the fourth and early third centuries was also an important intellectual capital of China. The current rulers of Qi, surnamed Tian, had usurped the throne from the descendants of Taigong Wang and over a century later were still seeking legitimacy for their reign. By the time of King Wei (reigned 356–32 B.C.) an academy had been established to enhance the kingdom's status as a center of innovative thinking. In those days wandering scholars, in the tradition of Confucius, traveled about the various states offering their strategies of war or schemes of policy to whatever ruler would employ them. King Wei and his successor, Xuan, welcomed these academicians, furnishing them with rank, retinues, luxurious residences, and remuneration. Indeed, King Xuan at one time boasted an academy of over a thousand philosophers. A great hall was constructed beneath Ji (Millet) gate at the west wall of the capital city of Lin Zi, and the academy henceforth adopted the name Ji Xia. One debate which was ongoing at the Ji Xia Academy at this time was the question: how do things come into being?[2] Two academicians named Ji Zhen and Jiezi took opposite sides of the debate, the former arguing the doctrine that "no one or nothing makes it," and the latter holding that "someone or something causes it." Nothing else is known about these two scholars, but it is evident that they were concerned with the same questions raised by Huang Liao and Zhuang Zhou.

As to the origin of *Tian wen*, the Oxford scholar David Hawkes believes it began as a shamanistic catechism,[3] while Columbia professor Burton Watson hypothesized that the questions represent a sort of storyteller's prompt book.[4] Both of these theories presume a multi-layered text, one that was conceived in a previous form and revised into a later more elegant or extensive shape. I am willing to admit the poem is not the product of a single poet. But instead of positing a priestly or popular origin, I offer instead an academic origin. The most plausible theory is that roving scholars from states such as Song and Chu gathered at Ji Xia under the patronage of King Xuan (r. 319–301 B.C.) and composed the poem as a group.[5] Only literati from the small state of Song, where the Shang dynasty royal house was settled after being conquered by the Zhou, could be expected to remain so conversant with obscure topics of Shang legend that make up a substantial portion of the section on human affairs. Indeed, the verses concerning Wang Hai, the domesticator of cattle and the ancestor of the Shang kings, were indecipherable from the Han dynasty onward until the discovery of Shang oracle bones in modern times.

The *Shi ji* (Records of the Historian) notes that the roving scholars of Ji Xia numbered several hundreds and thousands of men. Some of the most famous philosophers of the Hundred Schools resided here at one time or another, including Zou Yan, leader of the School of Yin and Yang; Shen Dao, a leading proponent of the Way of Huang (Di, or the Yellow Emperor) and Lao (Zi, the preeminent Taoist philosopher), otherwise known as the School of Taoism; and Song Xing, a member of the School of Storytellers. The topics of the *Tian wen* questions are so extensive that it seems unlikely one man could have devised them all. Instead, the disorganized and confused nature of their assembly points to a collective authorship. With a Zou Yan to inquire into the workings of *yin* and *yang*, a Huang Liao to question celestial phenomena, a Song Xing to provide illustrative tales and parables, a Song native to supply the legends of the Shang, a native of Lu to supply the Zhou legends, a man of Chu to provide anecdotal information from the South, and a Hui Shi or Gongsun Long, famous adherents of the School of Names, to organize the argument, it is possible to imagine how the poem might have taken shape. Since Qu Yuan is known to have made several journeys to Qi as envoy of Chu, it is also possible that he knew of the debate and offered arguments. Since the poem is traditionally attributed to him, it may be that he collected the fragments circulating at Ji Xia and produced the *Tian wen* as it was later anthologized. As to the purpose of this questionnaire, it may have begun simply as a debate exercise, created to give the popular and prominent dialecticians a tool for honing their convoluted responses.

In my translation I have adhered to the traditional order of lines, except for one instance where a rearrangement appeared to make some sense out of meaningless phrases. The division of the poem into three parts is traditional, appearing at least as early as the Tang dynasty, but different commentators divide the poem and rearrange its lines differently[6]. I have adopted the *pinyin* system of romanization for all but three Chinese words. For the tyrant and last monarch of the Shang dynasty whose name is spelled the same as the dynasty which overthrew him, I have used the Wade-Giles spelling "Chou" to avoid confusing him with the "Zhou" dynasty. In the case of Gun, the father of Yu the Great, queller of floods, I have chosen the Wade-Giles spelling "Kun" in order to avoid confusion with the English word "gun." Similarly, I have employed the name "Ho" to avoid the use of the *pinyin* spelling "he." For the reader's convenience a conversion chart of romanization systems is provided at the end of the Poem Notes.

[1] A. C. Graham, tr., *Chuang-tzu* (London: Allen & Unwin, 1981), pp. 49–50.
[2] Benjamin I. Schwartz, *The World of Thought in Ancient China* (Harvard University Press, 1985), p. 227.
[3] David Hawkes, tr., *The Songs of the South* (New York: Penguin Books, 1985), p. 126.

[4] Burton Watson, *Early Chinese Literature* (Columbia University Press, 1962), p. 246.

[5] Tan Jiefu, *Qufu xinbian* (Beijing: Zhonghua, 1978), p. 408.

[6] The translation is based on the *Tian wen* text of Hong Xingzu's *Chuci buzhu*, collected in the *Sibu congkan*. Commentaries consulted, in addition to Tan Jiefu, were Wen Yiduo, *Tianwen shuzheng* (Beijing: Sanlian, 1980); You Guo'en, *Tianwen zuanyi* (Beijing: Zhonghua, 1982); Huang Shouqi and Mei Tongsheng, *Chuci quanyi* (Guiyang: Guizhou Renmin, 1984); Cheng Jiazhe, *Tianwen xinzhu* (Chengdu: Sichuan Renmin, 1984); and Fu Xiren, *Xinyi Chuci duben* (Taibei: Sanmin, 1976).

PART ONE
THE PATTERNS
OF HEAVEN

曰

遂古之初誰傳道之

上下未形何由考之

冥昭瞢闇誰能極之

馮翼惟像何以識之

1

Of the beginning of old,
Who spoke the tale?

2

When above and below were not
   yet formed,
Who was there to question?

3

When dark and bright were obscured,
Who could distinguish?

4

When matter was inchoate,
How was it perceived?

明明闇闇惟時何爲

陰陽三合何本何化

圜則九重孰營度之

惟茲何功孰初作之

5

Brightest bright and darkest dark,
What was made from only these?

6

Yin and *yang*, blend and mix,
What was the root, what transformed?

7

The circular and nine-tiered Heaven,
Who enclosed and surveyed it?

8

Just how was this achieved?
Who originally made it?

斡維焉繫天極焉加

八柱何當東南何虧

九天之際安放安屬

隅隈多有誰知其數

9

Where is the Dipper tied with
    the Cord?
How is the Axis raised?

10

How are the Eight Pillars placed?
What is the Southeast Fault?

11

The Nine Heavens' borders,
Where do they reach, where touch?

12

Their edges and angles are many;
Who knows their number?

天何所沓十二焉分

日月安屬列星安陳

出自湯谷次于蒙汜

自明及晦所行幾里

13

What does Heaven tread upon?
How are the Twelve partitioned?

14

The sun and moon are how coupled?
How are the patterned stars ranged?

15

Emerge by the boiling canyon,
Arrive at the vale of night.

16

From light until dark
Is a pass of how many miles?

夜光何德　死則又育

厥利維何　而顧菟在腹

女歧無合　夫焉取九子

伯強伊慮惠氣安在

17

What virtue moves the moon
To flourish after death?

18

What good is it
To keep a rabbit in the gut?

19

From Nü Qi, the virgin,
Wherein came nine sons?

20

Where dwells Bo Qiang?
Where blows the auspicious wind?

何闔而晦何開而明

角宿未旦曜靈安藏

21

What closes and then darkness?
What opens and then bright?

22

Before the Horn has risen,
Where hides the Lord of Light?

PART TWO
THE PATTERNS
OF EARTH

不任汨鴻師何以尚之

僉曰何憂何不課而行之

鴟龜曳銜鮌何聽焉

順欲成功帝何刑焉

23

Kun was forbidden to quell the floods,
Why did the people choose him?

24

They said, "No need to worry,
Why not let him try?"

25

The Great Horned Turtles followed
     beak to tail.
What did Kun learn from them?

26

He began his task accordingly.
Why did Di then punish him?

永遏在羽山夫何三年不施

伯禹愊鮌夫何以變化

纂就前緒遂成考功

何續初繼業而厥謀不同

27

Banished forever to Feathered Crag,
Why, for three years, was he not
    released?

28

Yu was born from the belly of Kun.
How did the change transpire?

29

Taking up the original work,
The son completed the father's task.

30

How could he keep the prior plan
If his scheme was not the same?

洪泉極深何以窴之

地方九則何以墳之

河海應龍何盡何歷

鮌何所營禹何所成

31

Flood waters deep,
How were they filled?

32

The Nine Regions of the earth,
How were they arranged?

33

What did the Winged Dragon draw?
How course the rivers and oceans?

34

What site did Kun design?
What plan did Yu complete?

康回馮怒墜何故以東南傾

九州安錯川谷何洿

東流不溢孰知其故

東西南北其修孰多

35

When Kang Hui was enraged,
Why did the earth collapse in the
    southeast?

36

How were the Nine Lands blocked?
How did the rivers clog?

37

Their eastward flow never fills the sea.
Who knows why?

38

From East to West, South to North,
Which length is greater?

南北順陸其術幾何

崑崙縣圃其尻安在

增城九重其高幾里

四方之門其誰從焉

39

South to North runs long and
    narrow.
How much longer and thinner?

40

The Hanging Garden of Kunlun,
What does it rest upon?

41

Terraced walls of nine layers,
How many miles tall?

42

Gates of the Four Directions,
Who passes through them?

西北辟啓何氣通焉

日安不到燭龍何照

羲和之未揚若華何光

何所冬暖何所夏寒

43

Open up the Northwest Gate.
What wind blows through?

44

Where the sun does not rise,
How does the Torch Dragon flame?

45

Xi Ho yet to soar,
How does the *Ruo* tree shine?

46

Where is the winter warm?
Where is the summer cold?

焉有石林何獸能言

焉有虯龍負熊以游

雄虺九首儵忽焉在

何所不死長人何守

47

Where is the stone forest?
What beast can speak?

48

Where roams the Horned Dragon,
Bearing on its back the bear?

49

The nine-headed Hydra
And Shu Hu, where do they stay?

50

Where is there immortality?
What do the Long Men guard?

靡蓱九衢，枲華安居？
一蛇吞象，厥大何如？
黑水玄趾，三危安在？
延年不死，壽何所止？

51
The nine-jointed calamus,
And *xi* blossoms, where do they grow?

52
The snake that swallows elephants,
How big can it be?

53
Black Waters that darken the feet,
And Three Perils, where are they
    found?

54
Life is long here, and there is
    no death,
What is the end of longevity?

鯪魚何所鬿堆焉處

羿焉彃日烏焉解羽

55

Where dwells the Ling fish?
Where flies the monster, Qi?

56

Why did Yi shoot down the suns?
How did the crow feathers scatter?

PART THREE
THE AFFAIRS
OF MAN

禹之力獻功　降省下土四方

焉得彼嵞山女而通之於台桑

閔妃匹合厥身是繼

胡維嗜不同味而快鼌飽

57

Yu labored to fulfill his duty
And came down to search for
    lowlands.

58

How did he meet the Tushan maid
And lie with her in the mulberry?

59

He longed for a mate and wed her,
Whose body bore him a successor.

60

Why was his hunger unlike the rest,
Sated instead by a morning's delight?

敄代益作后辛然離釁

何敄維憂而能拘是達

肯歸躬蘏而無害厥躬

何后益作革而禹播降

61

Qi claimed the throne of Yi
And suddenly met with disaster.

62

How could Qi encounter danger
And still be able to flee?

63

All gave up their quivers of arrows
And no harm came to Qi.

64

Why did the reign of Lord Yi abate,
While the seed of Yu multiplied?

啟棘賓商九辯九歌

何勤子屠母而死分竟地

帝降夷羿革孽夏民

胡躲夫河伯而妻彼雒嬪

65

Qi danced in the presence of Di;
Nine dialogues they had, and nine
  songs sang.

66

Nurtured by the mother, how could
  he slay her,
Whose body lay shattered on the
  ground?

67

Di sent down Yi of the East
To alter the fortunes of Xia.

68

Why did he shoot the Duke of Ho
And elope with the Duchess of Luo?

馮珧利決封豨是躬

何獻蒸肉之膏而后帝不若

浞娶純狐眩妻爰謀

何羿之躬革而交吞揆之

69

With bow of pearl and jade
    thumb-ring
Yi shot the Heavenly Boar.

70

Why did the fat of sacrifice
Displease the exalted Di?

71

Han Zhuo wed Sable Fox;
The Dark Lady devised a plan.

72

How could Yi's arrows puncture hide,
While conspiracy easily foiled him?

阻窮西征巖何越焉

化為黃熊巫何活焉

咸播秬黍莆雚是營

何由并投而鮌疾修盈

73

Heading west on a perilous route,
How did he cross the crags?

74

Transformed into a yellow turtle,
How was his spirit revived?

75

Together they sowed the dark millet.
The reed marsh was reclaimed.

76

How could the people cast their seed
If the scourge of Kun was widespread?

白蜺嬰茀胡爲此堂

安得夫良藥不能固藏

天式從橫陽離爰死

大鳥何鳴夫焉喪厥體

77

White serpent in a swirling mist,
Why does it hover about the hall?

78

From whence came the auspicious pill
That could not well be hidden?

79

Heaven's Longbow, crosswise in
    the sky,
When the sun retreated, died.

80

Why did the Great Bird call,
And thereby lose its life?

蒲號起雨何以興之

撰體協脅廈何以膺之

鼇戴山林何以安之

釋舟陵行何以遽之

81

Ping Yi howled and the rains began.
How did he accomplish this?

82

Xie Feng formed the shape of Wind.
From whence came the antlered head?

83

The mountains rode on turtleback.
How did he arrange them?

84

To cross the land a boat was
    launched.
How did he proceed?

惟澆在戶　何求于嫂

何少康逐犬而顛隕厥首

女歧縫裳而館同爰止

何顛易厥首而親以逢殆

85

Han Ao was in Hu.
What did he seek at his brother's
    wife's door?

86

Why was Shao Kang running his
    hounds,
When the head of Ao went
    rolling down?

87

Ru Ai stitched his garments.
That night he stayed and lay with her.

88

Why did her head fall instead,
When he was to meet his doom?

湯謀易旅何以厚之

覆舟斟尋何道取之

桀伐蒙山何所得焉

妹嬉何肆湯何殛焉

89

Ao devised a layered armor.
How did he make it strong?

90

He capsized the boat of Zhen Xun
    state.
By what scheme was he finally
    caught?

91

To Mengshan, Jie lead a punitive raid.
What did he thereby obtain?

92

If Mei Xi had restrained herself,
How could Tang have vanquished Jie?

舜閔在家父何以鰥

堯不姚告二女何親

厥萌在初何所億焉

璜臺十成誰所極焉

93

Shun was lonely living at home.
Why did the father want an
    unwed son?

94

Yao did not seek the elder's approval.
How did he marry his daughters
    to Shun?

95

The beginning of the end,
How was it recognized?

96

A jade tower of ten levels,
Who was so extravagant?

登立為帝孰道尚之

女媧有體孰制匠之

舜服厥弟終然為害

何肆犬體而厥身不危敗

97

She ascended Heaven to rule as Di.
By what virtue did she rise?

98

Nü Wa had a serpent tail.
By what standard was her body
    formed?

99

Shun submitted to his brother.
Still the youth would do him harm.

100

Why did that brute of a brother
Always fail to trap him?

吳獲迄古南嶽是止

孰期去斯得兩男子

緣鵠飾玉后帝是饗

何承謀夏衆終以滅喪

101

In Gu Gong's day was founded Wu.
They settled in the Southern Wilds.

102

Who had hopes of going there
To seek for two men's heirs?

103

Adorned with flying swans and jade,
She was worshiped like Lord Di.

104

How was she entangled in the plot
That ended with the fall of Jie?

帝乃降觀下逢伊摯
何條放致罰而黎服大説
簡狄在臺嚳何宜
玄鳥致貽女何喜

105

Tang came down to tour the realm.
There he found Yi Zhi.

106

When Jie was banished for his crimes,
Why were lords and black-hairs glad?

107

In her jade tower was Jian Di.
Why did Di Ku supplicate?

108

A gift bequeathed by the Mystic Bird,
How did it please the lady?

該秉季德　厥父是臧
胡終弊于有扈　牧夫牛羊
干協時舞　何以懷之
平脅曼膚　何以肥之

109

Hai was heir to his father's deeds,
For Ji was a worthy lord.

110

Why in You Yi did he revel,
While his sheep and cattle grazed?

111

Danced for him the aegis troupe,
Why was he enraptured?

112

Plump, with no ribs showing,
Why did he get fat?

有扈牧豎云何而逢
擊牀先出其命何從
恆秉季德焉德夫朴牛
何往營班祿不但還來

113

In You Yi was a herdboy.
What prompted the encounter?

114

The lady rose, the lord was hit.
From whence came the command?

115

Heng was heir to his father's deeds.
How did he claim the docile kine?

116

Why go back to curry favor
And not again return?

昏微遵迹有狄不寧

何繁鳥萃棘負子肆情

眩弟並謠危害厥兄

何變化以作詐後嗣而逢長

117

Wei retraced his father's steps.
You Yi had no peace.

118

Why did birds flock to the brambles,
When the trusted son indulged
    his lust?

119

Corrupted too was the addled youth
Who imperiled the elder brother.

120

How was the path of guile averted,
And the line henceforth endure?

成湯東巡有莘爰極

何乞彼小臣而吉妃是得

水濱之木得彼小子

夫何惡之媵有莘之婦

121

The imperial tour of Tang
    turned east,
And came to the You Shen frontier.

122

How did he beg for the service of Yi,
And gain an auspicious wife?

123

In a hollow tree by the riverbank
The baby boy was found.

124

Why did the Lord of Shen dislike him
And send him off with the bride?

湯出重泉夫何辠尤
不勝心伐帝夫誰使挑之
會鼂爭盟何踐吾期
蒼鳥群飛孰使萃之

125

Tang was released from the
    Zhong Quan gaol.
For what crime did he serve?

126

Not intent on toppling the throne,
Who forced him to make that choice?

127

At dawn we converged and covenants
    were sworn.
Why did they meet us here?

128

Crows of vermillion, flocking by,
Who bade them gather here?

到擊紂躬叔旦不嘉
何親撲發足周以命以洛嗟
授殷天下其位安施
反成乃亡其罪伊何

129

A blow was dealt to the body of Chou.
Shu Dan was not happy.

130

After plotting revolt, why did he sigh
When the fortunes of Zhou
   were sealed?

131

To Yin was granted the rule of the
   world.
How was the throne of Yin bestowed?

132

Instead of flourishing the kingdom
   fell.
Their transgression, what was it?

爭遣伐器何以行之

北驅擊冀何以將之

昭后成遊南土爰底

厥利惟何逢彼白雉

133
Implements of war were mobilized
    for battle.
How was this accomplished?

134
They advanced together striking
    at Yi.
How were the soldiers deployed?

135
King Zhao commenced a royal tour,
And journeyed to the South.

136
What did he stand to gain
By seeking the rare white pheasant?

穆王巧梅夫何為周流

環理天下夫何索求

妖夫曵衒何號于市

周幽誰誅焉得夫褒姒

137

King Mu was an avid charioteer.
Why was he intent on touring the
    realm?

138

He made a circuit of the world.
What did he pursue?

139

A strange pair bore their wares
    to market.
What were they hawking there?

140

Who would King You have put to
    death
Had he not received Bao Si?

天命反側何罰何佑

齊桓九會卒然身殺

彼王紂之躬孰使亂惑

何惡輔弼讒諂是服

141

Heaven's mandate is not assured.
Who is punished, who succored?

142

Nine times Qi Huan convened
    the dukes.
His life was smothered nonetheless.

143

That stalwart King Chou of Shang,
Who led him into delusion?

144

Why did he loathe his high ministers
While engaging the sycophant?

比干何逆而柳沈之

雷開何順而賜封之

何聖人之一德卒其異方

梅伯受醢箕子詳狂

145

How did Bi Gan admonish his lord
And thereby gain a grave?

146

How did Lei Kai flatter him
And thereby gain a fiefdom?

147

The sages were of equal virtue,
Why were their outcomes so diverse?

148

Mei Bo was sliced and pickled,
While Ji Zi feigned insanity.

稷維元子帝何竺之

投之扵冰上鳥何燠之

何馮弓挾矢殊能將之

既驚帝切激何逢長之

149
Hou Ji was the first born son.
How did Shang Di favor him?

150
Cast out on the ice,
How was he sheltered by the birds?

151
How was his prowess with bow
    and arrow
The marvel that sustained him?

152
Di Ku was stunned, his actions drastic.
How did Hou Ji flourish there?

伯昌号衰秉鞭作牧

何令徹彼歧社命有殷國

遷藏就歧何能依

殷有惑婦何所譏

153

Bo Chang rose in the midst of
    decline.
He seized the whip and rode the herd.

154

How was the altar at Qi removed
And exchanged for the mandate
    of Yin?

155

The tribe pulled stakes and moved
    to Qi.
How were they able to follow?

156

Beguiling was the bride of Yin.
What cause was there for alarm?

受賜茲醢西伯上告
何親就上帝罰殷之命以禾救
師望在肆昌何識
鼓刀揚聲后何喜

157

Chou served Chang a Thyestean stew,
So the Western Duke appealed to
    Heaven.

158

How did Chang reach the presence
    of Di
Who sealed Yin's fate and showed
    no mercy?

159

Shi Wang was found in a butchery.
How did Bo Chang know him?

160

He sang a song of wielding knives.
Why was the duke so pleased?

武發殺殷何所悒
載尸集戰何所急
伯林雉經維其何故
何感天抑墜夫誰畏懼

161

Wu rose up and slaughtered Chou.
What need had he to worry?

162

He bore a body into battle.
What need had he for haste?

163

He hung by the neck from a tree.
Why did he take his life?

164

How was Heaven moved and earth
  aroused,
And who was terror-stricken?

皇天集命惟何戒之

受禮天下又使至代之

初湯臣摯後兹承輔

何平官湯尊食宗緒

165

August Heaven bestowed the
  mandate.
What were the words of warning?

166

King Chou reigned under Heaven
Until supplanted by another house.

167

Zhi was first a servant;
Later Tang obtained his counsel.

168

How did he end as minister to Tang
And his heirs bow to forebears of
  Shang?

勳闔夢生少離散亡

何壯武屬能流厥嚴

彭鏗斟雉帝何饗

受壽永多夫何長

169

Valiant Ho was the grandson of Meng
Who was driven away in his youth.

170

How did he rise up gallant in his
    prime
And spread his might throughout
    the land?

171

Peng Keng served his lord a pheasant.
How did Di partake?

172

Longevity he gained, everlasting.
How did he live so long?

中央共牧后何怒

蚕蛾薇命刀何固

驚女采薇鹿何祐

北至回水萆何喜

173

The Viscount of Gong took the reins
    of state.

What was the wrath of the king?

174

Mean creatures are the bees and ants.

Why is their power pervasive?

175

She was shocked to see them
    plucking bracken.

How were they nourished by a deer?

176

North they headed to Water Bend.

What joy awaited them?

兄有噬犬弟何欲
易必以百兩平無祿
薄暮雷電歸何憂
厥嚴不奉帝何求

177

The elder brother owned a vicious
    dog.
Why was it coveted by the younger?

178

A hundred chariots were presented.
In the end a title was lost.

179

Lost at dusk in a thunderstorm,
What sorrow awaited the king's
    return?

180

The boy in his prime was not
    employed.
What was sought by Di?

伏匿穴處愛何云
荊勳作師夫何長
悟過改更我又何言
吳光爭國又余是勝

181

Prince Sou fled to Cinnabar Cave.
Why did he cry out in anguish?

182

He realized the danger and averted it.
What else could he say?

183

The army of Chu was meritorious.
How long did victory last?

184

Then Ho Lü of Wu attacked the state.
How was he able to conquer our
   land?

何環穿自閭社丘陵

爰出子文

吾告堵敖以不長

何試上自予忠名彌彰

185

How did she frolic in the temple,
End up at the burial mount,
And later give birth to Zi Wen?

186

Reporting that Du Ao would not
    reign long,
How did he guess what his lord would
    want,
And thereby augment his fame?

田笠博士雅屬

丙寅新正 西蜀馬廷基 敬書

Inscribed for Dr. Tien Li on New Year's Day, Year of the Tiger, by Ma Ting-chi of Western Shu.

NOTES

6. "Consummate yin is freezing cold; consummate yang is burning hot. The freezing cold falls from heaven; the burning hot rises from earth. The two come together, coalesce, and all things are born therefrom" (*Zhuangzi*, "Tian Zifang").

7. To the ancient Chinese, the world was seen as a chariot, of which the square earth was the cart and the round heaven the canopy. Heaven has nine levels, the highest of which, in Ursa Major, is the dwelling-place of Shang Di, the High Lord.

9. The sun, moon and stars move about beneath the lowest level of Heaven which is supported at the polestar by the Heavenly Ridgepole, or Axis. The Cord, attached like a handle to the Dipper, describes a circle about the polestar as it pivots about the Axis, and is a seasonal indicator when it points to the Twelve (cf. note 13).

10a. Heaven is supported at its extremities by these eight mountains, beginning in the northeast: Square Earth, East-most, Wave Mother, South-most, Hobble Horse, West-most, Imperfect, and North-most.

10b. After Nü Wa had created Man (cf. note 98), the earth was peaceful until the water demon, Kang Hui, or Gong Gong, began to battle with Zhu Rong, the god of fire. Their fighting ransacked the earth. In a fit of rage Gong Gong toppled Imperfect Mountain, causing heaven and earth to fall together on the northwest. Ever since, heaven tilts toward the northwest and the earth toward the southeast, forming a gap between the two where the southeast meets the sea.

13. The Twelve were the cyclical mark-points which sectioned the celestial equator into twelve two-hour segments. These were further divided into the twenty-eight lunar mansions, marked by a reference star in each of twenty-eight zodiacal constellations.

14. "Coupling" is apparently ecliptical. "Patterned stars" are either reference stars in the zodiac or the "moving stars" (the five planets).

15. *Tang Gu* is where the sun resides before its trip across the heavens. There it bathes, causing the waters to boil. *Meng Xi* marks the end of the sun's journey.

18. When Chang E ate the pill of immortality, given to her for safekeeping, she ascended not to heaven, but only to the moon, and was thereby changed into a toad. The ancient characters for toad and rabbit were the same, and a variant of the myth has a rabbit in the moon pounding a mortar making the elixir of immortality.

19–20. Nü Qi and Bo Qiang are both deities. The former was worshiped by infertile women, and her constellation is the Tail, which has nine stars. Bo Qiang was god of the bitter northwest wind, and his constellation, the Winnowing Basket, bordered upon the Tail. The auspicious wind originates in the southeast. It is said that when the moon sits in the Basket, a great wind will blow.

22. The Horn is the star Spica in the constellation Virgo. Spica rises in the east on April 16th at sunset. This phenomenon marked the beginning of the new year in several ancient cultures. In the year 2400 B.C., Spica would have risen on approximately February 15th.

25. The Great Horned Turtle could call like a bird. Perhaps Kun discovered that they followed undetectable courses of shallow water. By following their calls as they surfaced for air he could map the underwater terrain and thereby know where to build his dikes. To accomplish his task of damming the floods, Kun stole a magic soil from Heaven, the *xirang*, or "damming dirt." Di discovered the theft and punished him with banishment.

28. According to some versions of the flood myth, Kun was banished by sage-king Yao for failing to quell the floods. On his way to Feathered Crag, he fell from a precipice and apparently died. For three years his corpse remained intact. Thinking an evil spirit inhabited the body, Shang Di dispatched a dragon to slice it open, whereupon Yu, the son, was born from the father's bowels. Kun then turned into a yellow turtle and dove into the abyss.

29–30. Tradition says that Kun failed because he built dikes, whereas Yu succeeded because he opened channels. However, earlier versions of the myth do not distinguish between strategies.

33–34. Kun sympathized with the people and attempted to stop the floods in order to alleviate their suffering. Unsuccessful, his son Yu was commissioned by Heaven to complete the task. The Winged Dragon was on loan from Shang Di. It employed its tail to draw the watercourses, while Yu followed behind excavating.

35. The floods are partly attributed to Kang Hui, the water demon, who was probably vanquished by Kun.

37. Cf. note 10b.

41. The Kunlun Mountains are a mythical range in the northwest, the supposed source of the Yellow River and earthly residence of the Yellow Emperor. The Hanging Garden, the tallest peak in this range, was perched high in the clouds, and appeared separated from the earth, floating in the sky. From the Hanging Garden one could reach the first level of Heaven.

44. Since heaven is round and earth square, there are four corners of earth that never see the heavenly bodies. In the northwest corner (beyond Imperfect Mountain) was the country of Nine Yin, in the middle of which stood the Torch Dragon. This fabulous creature, half serpent, half man, held a torch in its mouth to light the land.

45. Xi Ho, daughter of sage-king Shun, is the mother and charioteer of the ten suns. The *Ruo* is a tree in the far west on which the setting sun paints its final rays.

49. According to the *Zhuangzi* ("Yingdi Wang"), Shu was emperor of the Southern Sea aud Hu was emperor of the Northern Sea.

51. *Ping* (*acorus calamus*) and *xi*, a type of hemp, were thought to confer immortality.

52. According to the *Shanhai jing* (Classic of Hills and Seas), in the Southern Sea lived the *Ba* snake, which was 800 feet long, and whose body was green, yellow, red, and black. Three years after it had eaten an elephant, it would spit out the bones. When collected by man, these bones were said to be able to cure any disease of the heart or stomach.

55. The Ling fish was the dragon-fish mount of the shamaness Nü Chou. This amphibious creature was large enough to swallow a boat and purportedly could fly. Nü Chou attempted to bring rain when the earth was burning up, but was overcome by the intensity of the ten suns.

56. The ten suns of Xi Ho rebelled against their mother whose habit was to ferry one sun across the sky every day. One morning all ten of them leapt into the sky in defiance. Since the best of earthly mediums could do nothing to save the earth, Shang Di sent down the great archer Yi to aid the people. Yi nocked his great bow and shot at one of the suns. His aim was true and one of the flaming balls began trailing fire and flying haphazardly, scattering golden feathers in its path. When the object hit the ground, all were amazed to see a golden, three-legged crow.

57. Yu, the Great, was searching for possible watercourses.

59. Once when Yu (in the form of a bear) was pursuing his wife, she changed into a rock to elude him. Angry, he cried, "Return my son!" whereupon the rock burst open on its northern face as the son (Qi, which means "open") was born.

65. One modern scholar states that Qi performed a "halberd dance" and presented three maidens to Shang Di, while a Song dynasty scholar believes that Qi merely dreamed he visited Heaven. Actually both commentators are correct if Qi's dance transported him to Heaven in a shamanistic trance.

67. Myth and history are inextricably mixed in the character of Yi Yi. At once he is the great archer who shot down the suns, while also a mere chieftan from Yi (east of the Central Plain).

69–70. Feng Xi, or the "Heavenly Boar," was a constellation. Just as Shang Di was unhappy when Archer Yi shot the suns, so was he displeased when his boar was sacrificed.

71–72. Xuan Qi, the Dark Lady, was the wife of Kuei, unpopular ruler of Xia. Yi first assassinated Kuei, and then ascended the throne. Han Zhuo, Yi's favorite minister, bludgeoned his master to death with Xuan Qi's aid. A former minister of Kuei's eventually killed Zhuo and returned the rule of the Xia dynasty to the House of Yu (cf. note 88).

74. The original text reads "yellow bear," but the ancient ideographs for "turtle" and "bear" only differed by one stroke of the brush. So many commentators think the "three-legged turtle" is preferable to the "four-legged bear," which is substantiated in several other texts.

78. This question appears to treat the myth of Chang E. When Archer Yi shot nine of the ten suns, Shang Di retaliated by banishing him from Heaven. Yi obtained im-

mortality pills from the Queen Mother of the West, but entrusted them to the care of his wife, Chang E (cf. note 18).

79. According to a Qing dynasty scholar the text of this couplet describes a rainbow.

80. Perhaps this is a variant of the previous myth. Some have speculated that the Great Bird is Shang Yang, a water spirit in the form of a bird. When Shang Yang danced (and beat his wings), a deluge was forthcoming. Thus the dance, and thereby the call, may represent thunder.

81. Ping Yi was God of Thunder.

82. Xie Feng is another name for Fei Lian, the God of Wind, who had the body of a bird and the head of a stag. The oracle bone inscription for "phoenix" was often borrowed to indicate "wind" (both are pronounced *feng*); and in 1500 B.C., "phoenix" was written as a combination of the pictographs for "long-tailed bird" and "stag." The obvious conclusion is that "phoenix" was initially the Wind God.

83–84. As the Great Yu traveled in his boat about the flood inundated land, a giant sea turtle swam behind him, transporting the "mountain-making" *xirang* (cf. note 25).

85–88. After Han Zhuo murdered Archer Yi and took his wife, he had the father's corpse served up as a meal to the sons. Refusing to eat, they all starved to death. A son by the union of Zhuo and Yi's widow was named Han Ao. Ru Ai, on the other hand, was the widow of one of Yi's sons, and thus was the sister-in-law of Ao. Shao Kang was the son of the slain Xia ruler, also murdered by Han Zhuo.

It is said that Shao Kang and Ru Ai devised a plan to kill Han Ao in his sleep. But Ao eluded the sword of Kang, who decapitated Ru by mistake. Later, when the prince went hunting, he unexpectedly encountered the tyrant Ao and promptly lopped off his head.

91–92. To appease the conquering monarch, the state of Mengshan presented Jie, the last ruler of Xia (r. 1818–1766 B.C.), with two beautiful women. From then on he neglected not only his wife, Mei Xi, but also the affairs of state. Tang, the founder of the Shang dynasty, conspired with Mei Xi, and Jie was overthrown (cf. note 105).

93–94. Yao was a legendary sage-king who abdicated his throne in favor of Shun. (Shun in turn abdicated to Yu, queller of floods.) Shun was treated cruelly by his parents, yet he showed them great respect nevertheless, waiting on them hand and foot. Yao recognized this as the highest of virtues and presented both of his daughters to Shun in recognition of his filial piety.

95–96. When Chou, the last ruler of Shang (r. 1154–1122 B.C.), began to eat his meals with ivory chopsticks, his nephew, Ji Zi, recognized this as the first sign of profligacy. Thus he predicted his uncle's downfall. The jade tower was one story higher than the heavenly nine, a sure sign of arrogance and reason enough for the loss of his mandate.

98. Nü Wa was the sister and mate of Fu Xi, first of the ancient sage-kings (r. 2852–2737 B.C.). He is credited with the invention of writing, and she of marriage. The siblings were only half-human—they sported dragon tails—and Nü Wa

is best known as the creator of Man, whom she formed out of yellow clay. Some dynastic registers list Nü Wa as the second sage-ruler; others indicate that she was the first. Modern scholars speculate that remnants of her myth are evidence of an ancient matrilineal culture.

102. Gu Gong Dan Fu had three sons by different wives and favored the youngest, born after his tribe had migrated to Qi. When the duke was approaching death, the elder sons fled south and occupied the state of Wu. Later, when Dan Fu's great grandson, King Wu, had founded the Zhou dynasty, he sought the heirs of his grandfather's brothers. He found two cousins, one of whom remained as lord of Wu, and the other he enfeoffed in Yu.

103–104. These couplets describe Mei Xi, consort of Jie.

105. Yi Zhi, or Yi Yin, farmed in the wilds of You Shen. Tang heard of Yi's wisdom on his tour of inspection, and sought to employ him. But the duke of You Shen would not comply. Only when Tang agreed to marry the duke's daughter was Yi allowed to go with Tang (see couplets 121–122). Yi's first duty was to spy on Jie, so to make it look authentic, Tang drove him out of the capital in a shower of arrows. Three years later Yi reported to Tang that Jie was debauched and the people were restive. He also reported a dream, relayed to him by Mei Xi, that Jie had just experienced: In the sky were two suns—one in the east and one in the west. There was a struggle, and the western sun was victorious. With this intelligence, Tang led his troops around to the western border of Xia before attacking. Jie

fled before a blow had been struck and perished in the wilds of Ming Tiao.

106. The "black-hairs" are the dark-headed, dark-eyed masses, that is, the common people.

107–108. Jian Di ascended the nine-storied tower while her lord, the sage-king Ku (r. 2435–2365 B.C.), sacrificed to Shang Di, seeking the birth of a son. A swallow suddenly fluttered into her chamber, laid a tiny egg, then flew away. She swallowed the egg and became pregnant. Her child was Xie, the first ancestor of the House of Zi, future founders of the Shang dynasty.

109–120. Wang Hai, eldest son of Ji, lived around 2000 B.C., and is said to be the first domesticator of cattle in ancient China. The names of him and his son, Shang Jia Wei, are often invoked in early Shang dynasty bone oracles, which were inscribed on the shoulder blades of oxen. The brothers Hai and Heng were pasturing their herds across the river in the neighboring kingdom. When the duke found out he invited them to his court and treated them like dignitaries. Soon the luxurious life had fattened them. But the duchess also developed a prurient interest in the two stalwart youths. She first caroused with Heng, the younger, and then seduced Hai, the elder brother. When jealous Heng discovered his brother's deeds, he informed a palace guard, who proceeded to the brother's bed and chopped the body of Hai into eight pieces. The unfaithful duchess had already conveniently vacated the premises. When the death of Hai was announced, the duke banished

Heng, who fled to his homeland. He reported only that his brother had been murdered and the herds were lost (See hexagrams 34 and 56 of the *Yi jing*, or "Book of Changes"). Heng was made king, and he pledged to return and recover the livestock. Arriving in You Yi, he found the duke had forgiven him, so he stayed and resumed his intemperate lifestyle. When he did not return home with the cattle, his people installed Wei, the son of Hai, as king. Wei crossed the river and massacred the citizenry. His line endured, and the kings of Shang are descended from him.

121–122. Cf. note 105.

123. When the mother of Yi Yin was pregnant, she had a dream in which a god told her to flee the village when water overflowed her rice-hulling churn. Under no circumstances was she to look back. The following morning the dream came true, and after running only a few miles she looked back to see her village submerged in flood waters. As a result, she was changed into a mulberry tree. Later, when the duke's daughter was picking mulberry leaves, she discovered a baby in a hollow tree. This was Yi Yin, who grew up to be short and dark with a misshapen head and crooked back.

127. King Wu, son of Wen, convened a gathering of eight hundred dukes to ask for their allegiance in his plan to overthrow Chou. With contracts he promised them rank and territory, making three copies smeared with sacrificial blood and burying the third. This was the first use of covenants in ancient China; oaths were no longer suffi-

cient. The text of this question contains the first person pronoun, *wu*, "I" or "we," which means the couplet is written from the perspective of King Wu and his army, or the people of Zhou in general. A similar situation occurs in couplet 184, when the people of Chu (or a poet of Chu) seem to ask the question.

128. An auspicious omen, this flock of "firebirds" foretold victory for King Wu. In the text of the poem the name of the species of bird is also a color-word in Chinese, representing a spectrum from blue-green to black. But in this couplet the reference is to a particular mountain bird and not to a gray-colored fowl. It is the flame-like vermillion color of the flight of birds that was particularly fortuitous, for red represented the Zhou clan. See the "Zhou Annals" of the *Shi ji*.

129. When the Zhou forces attacked Chou in the Yin capital, the tyrant committed suicide. Arriving on the scene, King Wu filled the body with arrows and cut off the head. Shu Dan was the son of Wen and the younger brother of Wu, and is best known as Zhou Gong, the Duke of Zhou. King Wen, who initiated the revolt against Chou, and his son Dan were concerned about the impropriety of toppling a throne that was sanctioned by Heaven.

133. Ode no. 157 of the *Shi jing* (Book of Odes) praises the Duke of Zhou for his successful expedition to quell rebellion in the east. But the weapons carried by his soldiers —axes, adzes, chisels, and drills—were not conventional. Iron was unknown at this time, and aside from ceremonial

items and conventional weapons, bronze was also used to construct woodworking (but seldom farming) tools. It would appear that Zhou Gong's warriors, in the absence of metal weapons, armed themselves with any available bronze implement.

138. Imperial tours of inspection are being criticized here. Local populations were required to feed and support the royal entourage, which often impoverished them.

139. During the reign of King Xuan of Zhou (r. 827–781 B.C.) a children's song related how the fall of the dynasty would be caused by a bow of mulberry and a quiver of wicker (weapons of the common man). When Xuan heard of a peasant couple selling these items in the market, he sought to have them killed. He was unsuccessful, and in their flight from the city the couple rescued an abandoned child who grew up to be the nemesis of King You.

140. Bao Si was the ransom for her imprisoned and condemned master. According to legend she was the daughter of a slave-girl impregnated by a dragon. King You (r. 781–770 B.C.), the last ruler of the Western Zhou dynasty, made her his queen. You lavished such attention on Bao Si that palace defenses deteriorated, and the Dog barbarians were able to enter the capital and assassinate him.

145. Bi Gan was the virtuous uncle of decadent King Chou, who continually admonished his indulgent nephew. When the king was told that the heart of a sage has seven orifices, he cut out the heart of Bi Gan to see for himself.

149–150. Hou Ji was born when his mother trod on the footprint of Di. Sage-king Ku, the expectant father, presumably distrusted divine conception and attempted to kill the child by exposing it to the elements. But the prince was protected first by the cows and goats, then by woodcutters, and finally by birds. He grew up to impart the knowledge of husbandry to his followers, and is the first ancestor of the Ji clan, rulers of the Zhou dynasty. See ode no. 245 of the *Shi jing*.

153. Xi Bo Chang, or Chang, the Western Duke, was the ruler of the fiefdom of Zhou, located west of the Shang capital.

155. When the Di barbarians threatened to annihilate the tribe of Ji, Chief Dan Fu first offered them tribute in the form of silks, horses, and jades. They refused, desiring only territory. So Dan Fu gathered his people together and told them it made no difference whether they were ruled by him or the men of Di, that their lives were more precious to him than his territory. Thus he departed. However, one by one, the people gathered their possessions and followed him on his journey to Mount Qi, the cradle of Zhou culture.

159–160. Shi Wang, or Taigong Wang, was singing this song in the market:

> Down—chop, chop—the cow,
> Up—chop, chop—the crown!

162. Having no time to conduct proper funeral ceremonies for his deceased father, King Wu carried the corpse (or

perhaps just the spirit tablet) of King Wen in his war chariot as he rallied the dukes. King Wen (Bo Chang) was buried after the Zhou dynasty was founded, thus his posthumous title.

163. This couplet refers to Shen Sheng, son of Duke Xian (r. 676–651 B.C.), and heir to the throne of the Zhou state of Jin. The new queen, Li Ji, wished her own son to be heir, and falsely accused Shen Sheng of plotting to kill the duke. The prince committed suicide to show his innocence.

168. Zhi, or Yi Yin, was held in such high regard by the early Shang kings that his spirit tablet was placed in their ancestral temple. Thereafter his spirit was accorded sacrifice alongside his lord, Cheng Tang (cf. note 105).

169–170. King Shou Meng of the Zhou state of Wu had four sons. He favored the youngest and would have made Ji Zha his heir, but the youth deferred. So the throne went to Zhu Fan, the eldest, who immediately declared that after his death the kingdom would pass to each individual brother in turn. In the meantime, Ji Zha had renounced his title and become a farmer. When the third brother died, he fled the country, and Wang Liao, the eldest son of the last reigning king, assumed the throne. This displeased Ho Lü, first son of Zhu Fan. In 514 B.C., he had his cousin assassinated and occupied the throne. His exploits are the subject of couplet 184.

171–172. Peng Keng, or Peng Zu, was adept at raising livestock and was an early master of the culinary arts. But he is best known for his longevity, living through three dynasties to the ripe old age of 800. Sage-king Yao enfeoffed him in Peng Cheng, so "Di" in couplet 171 may refer to Yao, who lived to the age of 117.

173. King Li of Zhou (r. 878–827 B.C.) was driven into exile by a popular uprising. Gong Ho, Viscount of Gong, took over the task of government. After the old king died, the state was devastated by drought, and Gong Ho's house burned to the ground. The diviners determined that King Li had sent the catastrophe, so Gong Ho returned to his native fiefdom, resigning the throne to the crown prince Xuan. Only then did it rain again.

175. Bo Yi and Shu Qi, princes of the Shang state of Gu Zhu, abandoned their patrimony to join Xi Bo Chang. By the time they arrived in Zhou, Chang was dead and his son Fa (King Wu) was parading his father's corpse and making covenants against Chou. The brothers were disgusted at Fa's impropriety and retreated to Mount Shouyang, swearing "never to eat the grain of Zhou." There they subsisted on bracken until a woman reproached them, claiming the ferns were also "of Zhou." Most sources conclude with their subsequent starvation. However, one tradition relates that Heaven sent a white doe to suckle the two starving exemplars of righteous conduct.

177–178. In the state of Zhao (one of the seven Warring Kingdoms) good King Jian Zi became ill and lapsed into a three-day coma. After regaining consciousness he related a dream in which he stood in the presence of Di. Standing at the right hand of God was a boy who was being presented a dog. The dream was interpreted as indicating one of his sons would rule and thereby obtain the tutelage of the Dai nation, whose ancestor was the dog. The middle son, Xiang Zi, was chosen as heir, and when the kingdom passed to him, he arranged a marriage between his sister and the ruler of Dai. The bridal present from Zhao to Dai was the standard one hundred chariots. However, the bride then poisoned her husband according to plan, and King Xiang Zi appointed his elder brother's son as new ruler of Dai. This in turn displeased Huan Zi, the younger brother of the king. He chased his nephew out of Dai and took his place. But he died after only one year's reign, and the people rose up and executed his son, placing the exiled ruler back on the throne.

181–182. In the Zhou state of Yue, three successive rulers were assassinated by the people. Wang Zi Sou, heir to the throne, fled to a mountain cave to avoid the same fate. The people found him, smoked him out, and convinced him to mount the jade chariot. As he climbed on, he raised his face to Heaven and cried, "Oh Lord! Why can't I alone be spared!"

183. In order to make sense out of extremely cryptic phrases, I have reversed the original order of couplets 182 and 183. At least one modern scholar has done likewise.

185–186. According to legend, Zi Wen was born from an illicit union. The girl's mother discarded the baby, but it was suckled in the wild by a tigress. The child was retrieved and grew up to become the loyal minister of Xiong Yun of Chu. Du Ao was the elder brother of Xiong, and current Chu king. When he plotted to kill his younger brother, the latter fled north to Sui. Here Zi Wen advised his lord, who gathered an army, returned to Chu, and assassinated Du Ao. Xiong Yun then became King Cheng, and Zi Wen remained his most trusted advisor.

CHINESE ROMANIZATION SYSTEMS

Below are approximate English equivalents to the pronunciation of *pinyin* and Wade-Giles (in parentheses) romanizations.

CONSONANTS

b	(p)	as in be	p	(p')	as in pie
c	(ts')	as "ts" in its	q	(ch')	as in cheek
ch	(ch')	as in churn	r	(j)	as "j" in Jacques
d	(t)	as in do	s	(sz)	as in sew
f	(f)	as in fan	sh	(sh)	as in shore
g	(k)	as in go	t	(t')	as in toe
h	(h)	like German *nach*	w	(w)	as in wood
j	(ch)	as in jeep	x	(hs)	as "sh" in she
k	(k')	as in kite	y	(y)	as in yet
l	(l)	as in land	z	(ts)	as in zipper
m	(m)	as in man	zh	(ch)	as "j" in jug
n	(n)	as in now			

DIPHTHONGS

ai	(ai)	as in aisle
ao	(ao)	as "ow" in now
ei	(ei)	as in weigh
ie	(ieh)	as in yes
ou	(ou)	as in soul
ui	(ui)	as "way" in sway
ua	(ua)	as "wa" in wander
uo	(uo)	as "wa" in waltz

VOWELS

a	(a)	as in far
e	(e)	as "u" in duck
i	(i)	as in machine, or
	(ih)	as "ir" in sir (with zh, ch, sh, r)
o	(o)	as "a" in waltz
u	(u)	as in sue
ü	(ü)	as in French u